BLACKOUT

Rebecca Green
Illustrated by Mathew Hunkin

THOMSON

™

NELSON

Contents

1. Moving Out

As the last of the boxes were loaded onto the truck, I slowly walked around the house that had been my home for the last twelve years, eleven months, and sixteen days. It was an empty shell. I sat on the floor in my bedroom and stared at the marks on the walls where my posters had been. Maybe tomorrow another girl would be living here, putting up posters of her own.

Mom and Dad just didn't see it the way I did. They didn't understand that, to me, our house was just as much a part of the family as Jinx, our cat. Jinx wasn't that impressed about moving either. I knew he was going to be even less impressed when he had to get into his cat box for the long journey from Whitefish Bay to Toronto. Like me, Jinx hates travelling.

Mom put her head around the door. "Ready to go, Lucia?" she asked. Sometimes parents ask the most ridiculous questions. Of course I wasn't ready to go. I would never be ready to go. Wasn't it obvious?

I couldn't stop the tears from sliding down my face, even though the last thing I wanted was sympathy from Mom. If it weren't for her stupid job, we wouldn't be leaving in the first place.

Mom sat down beside me, but I wasn't in the mood for talking. "Ready," I muttered.

Downstairs, Dad was helping the movers lift the last few things into the truck. I smiled as I saw the barbecue grill disappearing through the doors. "What are we going to do with a barbecue in an apartment?" I asked.

"You never know," Dad replied. "It might
be useful." Mom and I looked at each other.
I figured Dad was going to find it tough moving
away from the country, too.

The moving truck wouldn't arrive at our new
apartment until the next morning, so we were
spending the night in a motel on the outskirts of
Toronto. Mom and Dad had suggested that we
eat at Pizza Palace on the way, but even that
didn't cheer me up.

I watched the countryside speed past and thought about the friends I was leaving behind. I'd known most of them since kindergarten. My best friend, Anita, had promised to e-mail me every day, but I knew it wouldn't be the same. The worst thing was that it was my birthday the following week, and I wouldn't be able to celebrate it with my friends.

2. Moving In

The next morning, we arrived at the apartment early. "Morning!" called Dad to a woman as we walked through the lobby. The woman nodded, but she didn't smile. "She must have got out on the wrong side of the bed!" Dad whispered in my ear.

It was hard to keep out from under everyone's feet while our things were being unloaded into the tiny apartment. Jinx yowled as I lifted him out of the car and took him into the building, but I didn't dare let him out of his box. He'd probably head home as fast as he could, and who could blame him? I hung around the lobby for a while, then I decided to take the elevator to the top floor and check out the view from the rooftop.

When I got to the elevator, a girl who looked to be about the same age as I am was coming out. "Hi!" I said.

The girl nodded and looked away as she walked past me.

"Do you live here?" I asked. "I'm moving into 11A today."

"11B, across the hall," muttered the girl as the elevator doors closed.

"Seems like everyone got out of bed on the wrong side," I thought.

Mom had told me that you could see the entire city from the rooftop. It certainly looked that way. I could see streets and buildings in all directions. The skyscrapers towered all around, and I could just make out Lake Ontario glittering in the morning sun between two of the buildings.

Even up here, I could hear the honking of car horns on the street below. I stood looking down at the rush-hour traffic and the people hurrying along the sidewalk.

By that evening, Mom and Dad had finished arranging the furniture. Everything looked cramped in the small apartment: the bookshelf was jammed in beside the sofa and we had to breathe in to squeeze past the dining room table.

"Hmm …" Mom frowned. "Maybe we'll have to buy some new furniture."

"I think it's cosy," said Dad. "By the way, Mrs. Krause from 12C just gave us a cake. She seems very friendly. In fact, everyone seems very friendly. I guess that's a bonus of living in a small apartment building."

"Why don't you unpack your boxes?" Mom asked.

"Not now," I said. "I'm going to watch TV for a while." I flicked through the channels, but there was nothing good on.

"Can I just watch the end of the news?" asked Mom as she sat down beside me.

I sighed and handed her the remote. "The government is warning that power outages could affect cities in Ontario again this year as…."

I tuned out and stared through the window at the city lights twinkling into the distance. My friends were hundreds of kilometres away, but I felt like I was on another planet. In the country, there were no twinkling lights at night, just the shadows of the trees in the darkness.

3. Birthday Blues

Mom had to start her new job right away, but I had another week's vacation before the beginning of the new school year. I usually hung out with Anita during the vacations. In the winter, we'd watch movies at my place, and in the summer, we'd ride our bikes down to the creek or play soccer in the yard.

This vacation there would be no Anita, no movies, no yard, and no creek. It was just going to be Dad, Jinx, and me, and Dad was busy setting up his new office in the study.

Jinx was as homesick as I was. We moped around the apartment together—neither of us was allowed to go out on our own in case we got lost. Jinx spent the first two days in his basket, refusing to eat.

"Come on, Jinx," said Mom, shaking a bag of his favourite cat treats, but he wouldn't budge.

On my birthday, Anita called to say hi.

"How's it going?" I asked her.

"Boring!" she replied. "I've got no one to talk to and nothing to do."

"Join the club," I said.

"At least you're in the city, though. That has to be better than hanging around here," she said. "So, what are you doing for your birthday?"

"Mom and Dad are taking me out for dinner and then we're going to a movie," I said. "I don't know anyone else around here."

We complained to each other for another fifteen minutes until Anita's mom told her to get off the phone.

"Lucia, we're leaving at seven," Dad called as he walked past my room, carrying a box of files. "Make sure you're ready!"

I put on my new sweater and brushed my hair as Jinx wrapped himself around my legs. He was the only one who understood what it was like to be stuck here all day.

Suddenly, the room went dark. Everything was silent, apart from the traffic outside. "Dad!" I called. "What's going on?"

I fumbled my way to the door as Dad emerged from his office. "Must be a fuse," he said. "Do you have a flashlight?"

I felt my way to my desk and found the flashlight I used for camping.

Dad opened the electrical panel in the hall. "Hmm, looks okay to me," he said. We made our way to the front door and peered out. The hallway was dark, and the elevator wasn't working. "I'd better check on Mrs. Krause in 12C. Why don't you turn on the radio and see if you can find out what's happening?"

I raised my eyebrows.

"Ah, yes, no electricity. Well, forget the radio," said Dad.

I went to the window and looked out across the city. It was a strange sight, almost as though I had been transported back to the country. Instead of the thousands of twinkling lights, the city was in darkness. Only the car headlights shone on the roads below.

Dad walked back along the hallway with Mrs. Krause just as the janitor, Mr. Williams, came through the stairwell door. "Don't panic," he said to the small group that was now gathered. "There's been a power failure. No one has electricity, but the authorities are working to get the power back on as soon as possible. Does anyone have a battery-powered radio?"

"I have," said Mrs. Krause. "I'll bring it out so everyone can hear it."

"Good. You'll be able to listen for updates," Mr. Williams said, and then he continued up the stairs to the next floor.

Suddenly we heard a small, nervous voice. "Tanisha?"

It was the woman from 11B, across the hall. Her pale face looked out anxiously. "My daughter Tanisha!" she called. "She went down to the basement to fetch the laundry, and she hasn't come back!"

"Don't worry, Mrs…." Dad trailed off.

"Marianne, call me Marianne," she said.

"Well, don't worry, Marianne," said Dad. "Your daughter will still be there. She just won't have been able to find her way back in the dark."

"I could go and look for her," I offered.

Marianne looked grateful. "We'll both go," she said.

"You can't go by yourselves," said Dad. Just then, Mr. Williams came down the stairs holding a toolbox. Marianne quickly explained about Tanisha.

"I need to check the switchboard," he said, "so I'll come too."

I told Dad we'd be fine. "Besides, I'm used to wandering around in the dark," I reminded him. "There are no streetlights in the country."

"All right," Dad said. "Just hold on tight to your flashlight."

4. Who's Afraid of the Dark?

We began walking down the stairs with my flashlight shining into the darkness. Voices echoed eerily up from the hallways as people gathered to discuss the power failure, and the noise of doors banging seemed to bounce off the walls.

I held onto the banister and shone the flashlight on the steps in front of me. The flights of stairs seemed to spiral downward forever. As we made our way down, the echoes became quieter and the air became colder.

When we reached the first floor, we crossed the lobby. Mr. Williams had set up a battery-powered lamp, and the dim light shone through the leaves of an enormous potted palm.

I pushed against the heavy doors that led to the basement stairs and screamed as a face appeared in the tiny window. The face screamed back.

The woman that Dad had passed in the lobby on the first day put her head around the door. "What are you doing?" she shrieked. "You scared me to death."

"Sorry!" Marianne said. "We're just going to the laundry room to look for my daughter."

"I haven't seen a soul down here," the woman said. "I can't see a thing!" She clutched her laundry bag tightly.

"Just wait here in the lobby," Mr. Williams said. "And don't panic! We'll be back once we've found Tanisha."

The stairwell was pitch black as we fumbled our way down the steps. At the bottom, I shone my flashlight to the left and right. There was no one in sight. To the right was the door to the parking lot and to the left the corridor led to the laundry room. I shone my flashlight down the corridor, and we began feeling our way along the wall. CLANG! My flashlight hit something metal, crashed to the floor, and went out.

"Are you all right?" asked Marianne.

"Sure," I replied, although it was really dark now.

Mr. Williams tried to reassure us. "Don't worry—I know my way around."

A strange gurgling noise was coming from the end of the corridor, and in the distance, there was a low rumble that seemed to be getting louder. Without my flashlight, this place had become really creepy.

"Let's try to find your flashlight," Marianne said.

I ran my hand over the floor. I edged forward on my hands and knees. After a while, the wall disappeared. Something brushed against my face as I put my head into an opening. I screamed and jumped back.

"Some birthday!" I thought to myself. I was beginning to wish I hadn't been so quick to volunteer to help. Then my foot knocked against metal, and something cold and wet soaked into my sneakers and jeans.

"Ugh!" I cried. "I'm all wet." Forgetting about the flashlight, I crawled along the corridor as fast as I could with Marianne following. Finally I came to a door, and I pushed it open.

"Tanisha!" I yelled.

"Over here," came a small voice from the back of the room. "Who's there?"

"It's Mom, Tanisha," Marianne said. "And Mr. Williams and Lucia from 11A. Are you okay?"

Tanisha shuffled across the floor and grabbed onto her mother. "It's spooky down here in the dark," she said. "Thanks for coming to get me."

"That's cool. It's no big deal," I replied.

"Was that you making all that noise out there?" she asked.

"Err … well, I dropped my flashlight," I explained.

As we felt our way back along the corridor, my foot kicked something hard—the flashlight!

21

I flicked it on and shone it back down the corridor. There was an overturned bucket beside the janitor's closet.

Mr Williams chuckled. "No damage done," he said. "Just take care on your way up."

When we reached the lobby, the woman who had screamed at me was waiting for us. Thankfully, she had calmed down. Tanisha grinned at me.

"What?" I asked.

She pulled me in front of a large mirror. My hair was covered in wisps from a spider's web, and my jeans and sneakers were soaking wet.

The three of us walked up the stairs to our floor. Then the woman hurried to her apartment to check on her cat. I found a note stuck on the door of my apartment: "Lucia, Marianne, and Tanisha, come up to the roof!" it read.

I frowned. What now?

"You'd better change your clothes first,"
Marianne said. "You can borrow a pair of Tanisha's
track pants. What size shoes do you wear?"

Tanisha showed me her room. It was
decorated with posters and photographs. "These
are my friends: Leah, Antonia, and Abbas," she
said, pointing at one of the photographs. "You
can come over on Thursday and meet them if
you like."

5 Moving On

"HAPPY BIRTHDAY!" Everyone jumped out at us as we followed a path of candles leading to the far end of the roof garden.

The evening breeze brought a delicious smell of hot dogs. "That's impossible!" I thought, until I saw burgers and hot dogs sizzling on the barbecue. The table was set with plates and cutlery. There was even a "Happy Birthday" banner.

"I told you the barbecue might come in handy," Dad said as he turned the burgers.

"Where's Mom?" I asked.

"I don't know," Dad said. "I've tried her cellphone, but it's not working. The radio says the subways are closed, so I expect she's had to stay at the office." He looked a little worried.

By eight o'clock, it seemed as though half the apartment building had joined us, even though it was only the people from our floor. Tanisha's mom was playing her guitar, and Mrs. Krause was demonstrating the waltz. Even the woman whom we'd met in the basement arrived and gave me a big smile.

"I'm sorry I gave you a fright before," she said.

"Likewise!" I said.

There was an odd collection of food that people had brought from their kitchens, such as half a banana cake, and a tub of melting ice cream—delicious. It was the best birthday party I'd ever had.

I was just helping myself to another hot dog when Mom arrived, looking exhausted. She threw herself onto a chair. "I've just walked all the way from Union Station," she said.

"You should have stayed at work," replied Dad.

"And miss my daughter's thirteenth birthday! Never!" she cried. "It looks like your evening out won't happen, though."

"I don't mind. I'd rather stay here anyway," I said.

"Well, I have something that is going to make you very happy," she added.

From her bag, she took a box wrapped in blue shiny paper. I slowly peeled back the wrapping and pulled out a cellphone.

"Wow!" said Tanisha. "That's cool!"

"Now you'll be able to text-message and send photos to your friends from time to time," said Mom. "Why don't you try calling Anita now?"

I tried to switch the phone on, but nothing happened.

Dad looked at the instructions on the back of the box. "You have to charge it first," he said.

"I'll go and plug it in … ah," I hesitated. "Well, it doesn't matter. I'll text Anita tomorrow when the power's back on. I'll be able to tell her all about the party."

The 2003 Blackout

At 4:11 p.m. on August 14, 2003, Ontario and much of the northeastern United States were hit by the largest blackout in the history of North America. Fifty million people were suddenly without electricity. That night, large cities such as New York and Toronto were so dark that you could see the Milky Way galaxy in the sky. Normally, the streetlights are so bright that you can't see any stars at all.

Just before the blackout, there was a surge in demand for electricity. Power lines were carrying so much electricity that they heated up and began to sag between the poles. In Ohio, in the United States, the sagging power lines brushed against tall trees and burned out. The main electrical system detected the break and cut the electricity off. Eventually, this caused many systems across Canada and the United States to stop working as well.

Some blackouts are caused by storms. Lightning, high winds, and heavy rain can damage electrical systems, and falling trees can get caught in power lines.

Blackouts remind us how easy it can be for a power grid to fail. Even the most well organized electrical system breaks down sometimes, so it's important that we know what to do when a blackout happens.

The blackout in New York

Electrical Power

When we flick on a light switch or turn on a computer, we don't usually think about how far the electric current has travelled. It reaches our homes through a complicated maze of lines and cables.

1. Electricity can be generated at many different sources, for example, a solar power station or a hydro-electric power station.

2. The electric current travels through thick wires called transmission lines. Tall towers called pylons link them together.

3. The transmission lines enter a major substation. Here, the voltage or force of the electric current is reduced so that the current is safe enough to travel along thinner power lines.

4. The electric current travels to a smaller substation in a town or city. The voltage is reduced again to make the electrical power safe for use in small factories, farms, and people's homes.

5. Electrical power arrives at your home along a thick cable that leads to a box called a meter. From the meter, wires called circuits run through your home. Each circuit leads to a power plug inside.

6. When you plug in a TV and switch it on, the meter works out how much electrical power is being used. This is how the electricity company knows how much to charge you.

DIGGING DEEPER

Keeping Safe in a Blackout

During a power failure, there are some important things you can do to keep safe.

▶ First, keep calm! It's best to stay at home with your family. It might not be safe to travel because traffic lights may be out and other transportation systems may have stopped running.

▶ If you have a battery-powered radio, turn it on. You can listen to information about what is happening and hear advice from officials. It's always helpful to keep informed.

▶ You should turn off all electrical appliances, such as the TV and computer. However, it's a good idea to leave a light switched on so that you'll know when the power is restored. When the light appears, wait for about fifteen minutes before you switch on anything else.

▶ If you're using candles, take care that you only burn them when people are in the room. Keep each candle in a holder so that it stays steady.

▶ Don't open the refrigerator or the freezer unless you really need to. Food can stay frozen for up to two days if the door is kept closed.